MW01121798

McCARTHYISM
AND THE
COMMUNIST SCARE
IN UNITED STATES HISTORY

★ KAREN ZEINERT ★

Enslow Publishers, Inc.
40 Industrial Road
Box 398
Berkeley Heights, NJ 07922
USA

http://www.enslow.com

Originally published as *McCarthy and the Fear of Communism in American History* in 1998.

Library of Congress Cataloging-in-Publication Data
Zeinert, Karen.
    [McCarthy and the fear of communism in American history]
    McCarthyism and the communist scare in United States history / Karen Zeinert.
        pages cm. — (In United States history)
    "Originally published as McCarthy and the Fear of Communism in American History in 1998."
    Includes bibliographical references and index.
    ISBN 978-0-7660-6345-7
    1. Anti-communist movements—United States—History—20th century—Juvenile literature. 2. McCarthy, Joseph, 1908–1957—Juvenile literature. 3. Internal security—United States—History—20th century—Juvenile literature. 4. Subversive activities—United States—History—20th century—Juvenile literature. I. Title.
    E743.5.Z45 2015
    324.1'3—dc23
                                                    2014025737
Printed in the United States of America

102014 Bang Printing, Brainerd, Minn.

10 9 8 7 6 5 4 3 2 1

Future Editions:
Paperback ISBN: 978-0-7660-6346-4
EPUB: 978-0-7660-6347-1
Single-User PDF ISBN: 978-0-7660-6348-8
Multi-User PDF ISBN: 978-0-7660-6349-5

To Our Readers: We have done our best to make sure all Internet addresses in this book were active and appropriate when we went to press. However, the author and the publisher have no control over and assume no liability for the material available on those Internet sites or on other Web sites they may link to. Comments can be sent by e-mail to comments@enslow.com or to the address on the back cover.

❂ Enslow Publishers, Inc., is committed to printing our books on recycled paper. The paper in every book contains 10% to 30% post-consumer waste (PCW). The cover board on the outside of each book contains 100% PCW. Our goal is to do our part to help young people and the environment too!

Illustration Credits: Enslow Publishers, Inc., pp. 17, 20; From File Unit: Prominent Personalities: McCarthy, Joseph R. Record Group 306: Records of the U.S. Information Agency, 1900–2003, p. 4; Library of Congress, p. 1.

Cover Illustration: Library of Congress

Cover Caption: Senator Joseph McCarthy in 1954

☆ CONTENTS ☆

Senator Joseph R. McCarthy answers Tydings Committee questions on March 14, 1950.

Chapter 1

A MOST UNUSUAL BEGINNING

In early 1950, Senator Joseph McCarthy, like many other Republicans, had been asked to give speeches commemorating Abraham Lincoln's birthday on February 12. McCarthy could not have realized that the speech he planned to give would have such dramatic results.

McCarthy was to make several appearances. After speaking in Wheeling, West Virginia, he was to appear in Salt Lake City, Utah; Reno and Las Vegas, Nevada; and Huron, South Dakota.

These cities were not important political sites, so McCarthy would have little—if any—media coverage. As a result, he did not work especially hard on his presentation. After gathering some general information, McCarthy and one of his speechwriters put together a rough draft.

McCarthy's speech was mostly about America's powerful foes—Communists, who believed that the welfare of one's country was much more important than individual rights. To build a strong country, Communists said that the government should decide what would be manufactured, which crops would be planted, and who should do what work. Communists were convinced that everyone should be like them, and they openly vowed to topple governments all over the world.

Wheeling, West Virginia

McCarthy spoke to about three hundred people in Wheeling. His presentation was covered by a local news reporter, Frank Desmond, and an engineer from the radio station WWVA, who was taping the speech so that it could be played on the air later that evening. The senator's exact words, however, will never be known, since he was not reading from a text. Also, as usual, the tape reel was erased after its broadcast so the tape could be used again.

McCarthy said there was a dangerous situation in America: There were Communist spies in the State Department. This department has many important duties, including negotiating treaties and agreements with foreign nations. Since the audience had heard such statements before, this did not cause much excitement. When McCarthy announced that he could name the Communists, however, everyone listened carefully. Waving a fistful of papers, he said—as nearly as anyone could recall:

> I have here in my hand a list of two hundred and five [people] that were known to the Secretary of State as being members of the Communist party, and who, nevertheless, are still working and shaping the policy in the State Department.[1]

Reactions

McCarthy's words made headlines in the *Wheeling Intelligencer* the next day. The article was then picked up by the Associated Press, which sent copies to newspapers across the country. As a result, the senator's claims spread quickly. When McCarthy reached Denver on his way to Salt Lake City, eager reporters were waiting for him. They begged to see the list. McCarthy offered to give them a glimpse, but he could not locate the list in his briefcase. Disappointed reporters took photographs of the senator searching through his notes.

When McCarthy arrived in Salt Lake City, more reporters surrounded him, clamoring for names. Now he began to change his story. He claimed that there were fifty-seven Communists in the State Department. When asked for names and details, McCarthy refused to answer any more questions.

No one was more surprised at the attention paid to the Wheeling speech than Joe McCarthy. Later he confided to J. Edgar Hoover, the head of the Federal Bureau of Investigation (FBI), "This caused headlines all over the country, and I never expected it, and now I need some evidence to back up my statement that there are Communists in the State Department."[2] So the search for Communist sympathizers began, spawning one of the most frightening and controversial periods in American history: the McCarthy era.

RED SCARES

America's deep-seated fear of communism began on November 7, 1917, when the Russian government was seized by Communists. This highly disciplined group, with only eleven thousand members, was led by Vladimir Lenin.

Revolutionary Program

The Communists promised the Russians "land, peace, and bread."[1] This sounded good to poor, war-weary, hungry Russians who had suffered incredible losses in World War I, then in its third year.

Lenin's first step toward fulfilling his promise was to withdraw Russian soldiers from the front, ending his country's participation in the war. Lenin opposed international wars. He believed that they were fought by poor soldiers for the benefit of powerful leaders and industries that produced war materials such as weapons and tanks for huge profits. Instead of fighting the poor from other countries, Lenin said, workers should unite and revolt. Lenin believed the real enemy was the wealthy class, who had long benefited from labor's toil and low wages. To symbolize the violent revolutions that Lenin hoped would come and the common blood workers shared, the Communists used the color red in their banners. The color became so closely associated with the group that members became known internationally as "Reds." (Those who sympathized with communism, but were not Communists themselves, were called "Pinks.")

Lenin's withdrawal from the war was popular in Russia, and it won him support. However, Russia's allies— Great Britain, France, and America—were appalled. They saw Lenin's move as a betrayal.

The Communist party then set out to fulfill Lenin's promises of land and bread in ways that had never before been attempted on such a large scale. Drawing from ideas developed by Karl Marx and Friedrich Engels, who published the *Communist Manifesto* in 1848, Lenin claimed all the land in Russia for the government. He divided some of this land into small plots and granted its use and livestock to the peasants. Wealthy landowners whose estates had been seized were understandably upset by this action.

The Communists then took over the factories and set wages. No longer would factory owners become wealthy while laborers struggled to pay their bills. The Communist party also took over banks and railroads.

Then the party seized church property and tried to close all places of worship. Lenin thought religion was a distraction. What was important now, he argued, was the welfare of the state. Spending time on any task that did not benefit the nation was not acceptable.

Lenin's followers also took charge of the newly formed councils, regional governments that had been established only months before the revolution. These councils, called "soviets," gave the country its new name, the Soviet Union. The original purpose of the councils had been to give Russians a voice in their government. Now, to keep dissent to a minimum, the soviets were ruled by Communist party members.

In addition, the party organized a special police force to identify and arrest opponents. Lenin believed that he had to rule with an iron hand until the people had seen the advantages of communism. Then, ideally, everyone— men and women of all races—would be equal and so content that little government oversight would be needed to maintain law and order.

Opposition

Not everyone was happy with Lenin's leadership. Some Russians, and most Americans, considered communism little more than a godless dictatorship. Opponents began to organize shortly after Lenin took over. In 1918, a group known as the "Whites" tried to seize the government. The Whites wanted a more democratic leader. They were supported by many former landowners. The result was a civil war.

When the Whites rose in revolt, the United States, France, Great Britain, and Japan—allies of Russia in World War I—gave them limited help. These countries sent troops to northern Soviet seaports, infuriating Lenin. Even with outside help, though, the Whites were no match for the Reds. The Communists ruthlessly cut down their enemies, including several hundred American soldiers. The Reds won battle after battle, becoming more powerful by the day. When Lenin shook his fist in anger at the invading nations and vowed to conquer the world, free people everywhere took notice.

Red Scare in America

Lenin's threat terrorized Americans and started what is known as the first Red Scare. It lasted for seven years and grew more intense each year. By late 1919, the German and Italian Communist parties had many supporters, and party members in Hungary had actually taken control of their country for five months. In addition, Soviet agents had founded successful Communist parties in other European countries. Their job was to bring about the downfall of foreign nations in the hope that these countries would become part of the Communist world.

Meanwhile, in America, angry union members went on strike in large numbers. They, like all workers during World War I, had agreed to remain on their jobs until the conflict was over. As soon as the fighting ended in November 1918, unions sought higher wages and better working conditions. When negotiations broke down, workers went on strike. This was hardly a new idea.

The sheer number of strikes, however, alarmed the public. Americans were well aware of Lenin's statement urging workers to revolt. The fact that some of the strikes were led by men who voiced ideas similar to those held by Communists did little to calm the public's nerves.

Violent acts further alarmed the public. A bomb plot that targeted sixteen American anti-Communists was uncovered on May 1, 1919. That same day, violence broke out at May Day parades held in honor of workers in Cleveland, Ohio; Boston, Massachusetts; and Detroit, Michigan. There was also a violent incident in Chicago, Illinois. When some workers replaced an American flag with a red banner to symbolize a potential Communist revolution, a fight broke out between the workers and spectators.

In August, the Socialists caused more anxiety for the public. The Socialist party, which shared some of Lenin's beliefs—opposition to international wars, for example—split. After heated debates about how best to change America, some Socialists withdrew their membership, stormed out of the meeting, and formed two Communist parties. These were legitimate political organizations, which could recruit members at will.

Now Americans felt besieged. They not only faced a powerful enemy abroad, but also had Communist parties in their backyard. Remembering that it took only a few Communists to bring down the Russian government, Americans now believed their freedom was in peril.

The parties that Americans feared, however, were very weak. Even after they united and became the Communist Party of America, they were so deeply divided on how best to make the United States into a Soviet America that most of the members' energy was expended arguing among themselves. Some members were intent on changing America's political system with force. Most, though, wanted to change America through peaceful means. These Communists campaigned for candidates, usually Democrats and Progressives, who supported workers. In 1924, party members would begin to run nominees of their own, including candidates for the presidency.

By late 1919, the majority of Americans believed that all Communists were a threat. The public insisted that the federal government take action. The U.S. government responded by trying to remove the problem. On November 7, 1919, government agents rounded up hundreds of suspects. Approximately two hundred fifty of these were identified as dangerous. Eventually they were put aboard a ship dubbed the *Soviet Ark* and sent to the Soviet Union.

Strikes and protests continued, however, so another roundup of suspects was deemed necessary. In 1920, authorities arrested more than ten thousand radicals— Communists, Socialists, and anyone else who held very different beliefs from typical Americans. Unlike the first roundup, many of those arrested were United States citizens. Although many Americans applauded this act, some people began to question it. They accused the government of going on a witch-hunt.

Stalin Becomes Leader of Soviet Union

Joseph Stalin became the leader of the Soviet Union when Lenin died in 1924. Unlike Lenin, Stalin seemed determined to concentrate on affairs within the Soviet Union rather than spread communism throughout the world, at least in the immediate future. Believing that American Communists would receive little—if any—help from Stalin, the public thought that the Communist threat was no longer the serious problem it had been in 1919 and 1920. This marked the end of the first Red Scare.

New Fears

However, the relief that Americans felt was short-lived. In 1929, an economic crisis affected most of the world. Known as the Great Depression, the stock market crash and financial collapse of many businesses threw millions out of work. As a result, many began to question America's economic system. More than one person thought that it should be dramatically changed.

American Communists saw an opportunity to convert the public, so party members became more active than ever. They established schools to teach volunteers how to "colonize" an organization, and they set out to help the less fortunate to show what the party could do. For example, Communist writer Howard Fast helped workers by organizing them into unions and associations "that fought for lower rents, better living conditions, protection against landlords, better schools, and other neighborhood needs."[2]

The recruiters were very effective. Thousands of Americans joined the Communist party. Members included the poor, who thought the present economic system was unfair, and minorities, who admired the Communist dream of equality. New members also included idealists who were drawn by the promise of world peace.

The growing number of Communists convinced the public that a revolution was possible. This belief was so widespread that as one Communist later said, only one group "was . . . absolutely convinced of the impossibility of a Communist revolution in America—the members of the Communist Party."[3] The party never won more than one hundred thousand votes in any presidential election. More than half of these votes were from sympathizers. Even at its height, the party had no more than thirty thousand members.

Nevertheless, to stop any threat to the government, the House of Representatives created the House Committee on Un-American Activities (HUAC) in 1938, first headed by Congressman Martin Dies.

Before long, the committee announced that labor unions, the government, and the movie industry, which, according to Dies, put out Soviet propaganda disguised as entertainment, had all been infiltrated by Soviet agents. It did not matter if the Communists were committed to violence or preferred a peaceful means of changing the government. Communism, Dies said, was a threat to America. Period.

Afraid of what lay ahead, almost all Communists went underground, living under false names. They were dismayed when Congress passed the Hatch Act in 1939, which made it illegal for the government to hire Communists. Most were afraid others would follow suit, making it impossible for party members to find work.

World War II

Before the fear of communism created another full-blown Red Scare in America, World War II broke out in Europe. The war, which would last from 1939 to 1945, made the Nazi menace seem even more dangerous than any threat communism presented. Using terror and mass murder, the Nazis tried to take over territory, eliminate their enemies, and oppose both communism and democracy. Because of the Nazis' terrible methods, anyone fighting against Nazi Germany and its allies received support from America—even Communist nations. When the United States entered the war and became an ally of the Soviet Union on December 7, 1941, there was little outrage about fighting on the same side as the Communists. Americans believed the Nazis had to be stopped.

Second Red Scare

When the war ended, old fears returned in full force, resulting in a second, more traumatic, Red Scare. This was due, in part, to the rapid expansion of Communist territory in Europe and Asia after the war.

World War II allies Great Britain, France, the United States, and the Soviet Union had agreed that all four countries would share in the defeat of the Nazis. The Allies had also agreed that the countries conquered by the Nazis would become independent again after the war ended. However, when the time came for the Allies to withdraw, the Soviets refused to do so. The Soviet Union had defeated Nazi soldiers in most of Poland, Czechoslovakia, Romania, Bulgaria, Hungary, and eastern

Atlantic
Ocean

SWEDEN   FINLAND

NORWAY

DENMARK

IRELAND

UNITED
KINGDOM

SOVIET UNION

NETH.

W.   E.
GERMANY   POLAND

BEL.

LUX.

CZECHOSLOVAKIA

SWITZERLAND   AUSTRIA HUNGARY

FRANCE

ROMANIA

YUGOSLAVIA
(Independent
Communist
State)

PORTUGAL

ITALY

BULGARIA

SPAIN

ALBANIA

GREECE   TURKEY

Mediterranean
Sea

COMMUNISM DIVIDES EUROPE

East European satellites
of the Soviet Union

After World War II, Communists gained control of Eastern Europe and installed puppet governments, identified as East European satellites on the map.

Germany. It had occupied these countries to prevent the Nazis from controlling the territory. After the war, the Soviet Union would not give up its control. Instead, it installed puppet governments, run by leaders the Soviets could control. The refusal to honor withdrawal agreements made the Soviets appear untrustworthy and dangerous.

In addition to extending its power in Europe, the Soviet Union had gained land in the East by agreeing to enter the war against Germany's ally, Japan, in 1945. Through various treaties, the Communists had gained control of the southern part of Sakhalin Island and the Kurile Islands, as well as territorial privileges in Manchuria and the Korean peninsula. This would make it possible for the Soviets to eventually install Communist governments there.

Though the Soviets and Americans (as well as the rest of the free world) were not exchanging fire, they were so at odds over the Soviet expansion and the spread of communism that it seemed as if they were at war. This estrangement became known as the Cold War.

Communist Gains in Asia

At the same time, the Soviets were supporting a determined Communist party in China. China had been in turmoil since the end of World War I. The Chinese Communist party, led by Mao Tse-tung, was battling an American-backed government, led by Chiang Kai-shek.

Although a cease-fire had been in effect between the two forces during World War II, fighting between the Communists and Chiang Kai-shek's troops resumed as soon as the peace treaty was signed and the threat of Japanese attacks were over. By early 1949, it was clear that Mao's troops were winning the civil war. Many who backed Chiang Kai-shek accused the American State Department of failing to give him the weapons and support he needed. When Chiang Kai-shek and his troops were driven out of mainland China to an island now called Taiwan, opponents of communism accused the State Department of betraying the Chinese people.

The State Department pointed out that it had supplied military advice and massive shipments of weapons. Still, Chiang Kai-shek's troops had fought poorly or deserted as soon as the enemy was in sight. Short of sending American soldiers to China, there was little more that the United States could have done to prevent a Communist victory.

Measuring Loyalty

Americans were aghast when they looked at a world map and realized how much land was in the hands of the Communists. The American people began to look for a scapegoat—someone to blame. As early as 1946, many began to question the loyalty of government employees, especially those in the State Department who helped negotiate treaties with the Soviets after World War II. Were there, the public wondered, Soviet agents in government positions?

To lessen criticism and get rid of any disloyal Americans, the government, led by President Harry Truman, established loyalty boards in 1947. These boards

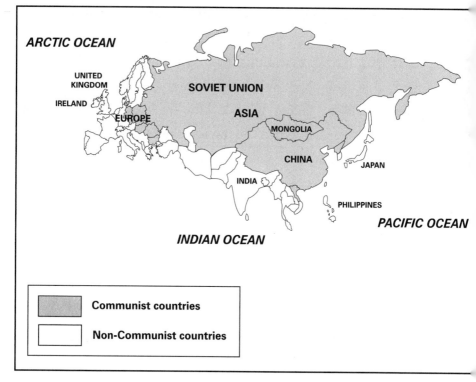

Communism spread throughout much of Asia in the early 1950s.

were supposed to identify anyone who might be a threat to United States security, especially Soviet spies.

Program administrators gathered every scrap of information they could find and listened to every rumor anyone was willing to repeat. Administrators encouraged informers, whose identity would be kept secret, to appear before loyalty boards.

Critics of loyalty programs accused the government of denying Americans their basic rights. These opponents pointed out that the Sixth Amendment to the Constitution guarantees the right of the accused to face his or her accuser. The First Amendment, they added, granted American citizens the right to hold any belief, even a belief in communism. Nevertheless, by 1952, the loyalty of more than 6.6 million government employees was challenged and evaluated. Of these, about five hundred were dismissed. Another five thousand quit their jobs rather than be subjected to an examination.

Soviet Threats and Spies

In 1949, Americans learned that the Soviet Union had atomic weapons. How, the stunned public wondered, had the Soviets accomplished this technological feat so quickly? They had been years behind America in developing such weapons. In a national poll taken in the late 1940s, 76 percent of the people polled believed that the Soviet Union was out to rule the world, and "63 percent expected a full-scale war [with the Soviet Union] within the next twenty-five years."[4] Although this was very frightening, Americans had counted on their superiority in weapons to give them an advantage if war should occur. Overnight, this advantage had disappeared.

Many Americans were so afraid of a nuclear attack that they began to take steps to protect themselves. Some built bomb shelters in their backyards. These shelters were stocked with food and water so that inhabitants could survive in them for a long period of time. Schoolchildren were shown how to take cover under their desks, should an attack occur during the school day. When government analysts listed the sites most likely to be hit if the Soviets attacked—large cities and armed service bases—some people actually moved. The atmosphere in the United States became one of intense fear and near panic.

Communist Spies at Work

While Americans were reeling from Communist gains on land and in science, several Communist spies were unmasked in Great Britain, Canada, and the United States. The most dramatic case in America involved Alger Hiss, a high-ranking employee in the State Department who had been an advisor at the convention of the Allies during World War II where Stalin had been promised land in Asia. Hiss was accused of working for the Soviet Union in the 1930s by Whittaker Chambers, a former American Communist. It was too late to prosecute Hiss for spying, since the statute of limitations had run out. Instead, HUAC prosecutors gathered enough evidence to convict him of perjury (lying in court). His conviction, only weeks before Senator Joe McCarthy gave his speech in Wheeling, made headlines.

At the same time, Dr. Klaus Fuchs, who had worked on atomic research in the United States during World War II, was being investigated. Fuchs was arrested in England on February 3, 1950, charged with passing along information about atomic weapons while he was working in the United States. This, in part, explained how the Soviets had developed the atomic bomb so quickly.

Fuchs confessed to spying for the Soviets, one day after McCarthy claimed he could identify more than two hundred Communists in the State Department. Fuchs also said that he could identify a number of high-ranking Americans who were at that very moment spying for the

Soviets. Fuchs's comments backed up McCarthy's claims, and as a result, McCarthy's speech took on special importance. Urged on by old fears, the Hiss case, and Fuchs's confession, Americans were ready to wage war on communism. They could not have found a more willing warrior to lead them into battle than Joe McCarthy.

TAILGUNNER JOE

Shortly after Senator Joseph McCarthy made his dramatic accusation, reporters scrambled to find out more about the man making the charges. Surely, they thought, such a man must have an unusual background. In many ways he did.

Early Life

Joseph "Joe" Raymond McCarthy was born in Grand Chute, a rural township in northeastern Wisconsin. Although various dates for his birth have been given, including several by McCarthy himself, official records indicate that he was born on November 14, 1908. He was one of seven children.

Joe's parents, Timothy and Bridget Tierney McCarthy, owned a 142-acre farm. They raised oats, corn, cabbage, and dairy cattle. The farm was successful enough to provide the basic necessities for the family, but few luxuries.

Biographers often mention that Bridget saw something in Joe that set him apart from her other children, all of whom would lead quiet, ordinary lives. She might have been influenced by his dreams of greatness. His sister Anna Mae recalled that Joe always wanted to do something big.

Joe and his brothers and sisters went to school in a one-room building. As was the custom then in farming districts, the McCarthys attended school through eighth grade, after which they worked on the family farm. Joe was smart and willing to work hard. He was also restless. He had unlimited energy and seldom needed more than a few hours of sleep each night. Eager to finish school, Joe completed his assignments for his last two years in only one year.

When Joe left school, he earned extra money by working on his uncle's farm. Then he bought chickens with this money. By the time he was sixteen years old, he had a thriving poultry business. He delivered crates of eggs and freshly butchered chickens to stores throughout the area.

About two years later, his business failed when he contracted a serious case of influenza. Unable to work for more than two weeks, he hired several boys to tend his chickens. However, the boys did not do a good job, and most of Joe's fowl died. Rather than start over he abandoned farming forever.

Running the Store

McCarthy then headed to Appleton, Wisconsin, where he found a job as a clerk in a Cash-Way grocery store. He loved to talk, and even though he had a nervous giggle and sometimes stuttered, he was popular with customers.

McCarthy soon became a Cash-Way manager, first in Appleton, then, in 1929, in nearby Manawa. There, he walked up and down country roads to personally invite local farmers to shop at his store. One customer recalled, "I never saw anybody so steamed up. He just couldn't ever relax; he worked at everything he did. He was pushing all the time."[1] His efforts turned Cash-Way's smallest store into its biggest moneymaker.

Back to School

Still, running the most profitable store in the chain was not enough for Joe McCarthy. He decided to return to school to get his high school diploma. At first, the high school principal in Manawa was hesitant to put the nineteen-year-old McCarthy into classes with young teenagers, who might tease him. However, McCarthy did not see this as a problem. He had met most of the students in his store and got along well with them. Besides, he was not going to be around for long. He planned to complete high school as quickly as possible.

At that time, Little Wolf High School allowed students to work at their own pace. They chose their own level of study, picking assignments that would earn an A, B, or C when completed. McCarthy usually chose A-level assignments. He worked at his typical frantic pace, completing grades nine and ten the first semester and grades eleven and twelve by early June.

On to Marquette

After receiving his diploma, McCarthy decided to go to college. Although he had some money saved, he did not have enough for all his college expenses, so he borrowed money from his brothers and his father. He enrolled in engineering classes at Marquette University in Milwaukee, Wisconsin. When engineering failed to hold his interest, he switched to law.

To help pay his college costs, McCarthy took on any and all odd jobs that he could find. This was during the Great Depression, when few jobs were available, yet he always managed to find something to do. At various times, he was working up to eighty hours a week in addition to going to school full-time.

McCarthy also began to gamble, playing poker with classmates for fun and profit. He loved to bluff. He would bet on his hand before he looked at his cards or bid lots of money on a poor hand just to see if he could force the other players to pull out.

While in college, McCarthy participated in several extracurricular activities, including debate. It was during heated debates that he began to show a side of himself that had not been obvious before. Whenever someone questioned his statements, he acted as if he had been personally attacked. Instead of his typical friendliness, McCarthy would become very angry. He lashed out at his challengers, often in a very disorganized fashion. McCarthy noticed how quickly his attacks quieted his opponents, many of whom were simply too stunned or confused to reply. From then on, he often resorted to verbal assaults to try to silence anyone who opposed him.

The reasons for McCarthy's angry, even mean-spirited, outbursts are not clear. Most historians believe that he was very insecure. As a result, he defended himself in such a way that everyone would think twice about questioning him in the future.

A Small-town Lawyer

After McCarthy received his law degree in 1935, he opened an office in Waupaca, Wisconsin. Few people took their legal concerns to this newcomer. In fact, he earned more money playing poker than he did representing clients. As a result, when an overworked lawyer from nearby Shawano, Mike Eberlein, asked McCarthy to join his firm in 1936, McCarthy jumped at the chance.

He worked with Eberlein for more than two years. During this time, Eberlein taught McCarthy some of the finer points of the law and supported him any way that he could. They were, Eberlein thought, good friends. In 1938, however, just before Eberlein was about to announce his candidacy for a circuit court judgeship, his long-time dream, McCarthy entered the race. Eberlein then decided not to run. Thirty-year-old McCarthy campaigned hard, talking to as many people as he could. He won the position by more than four thousand votes, a stunning upset for a relatively unknown, inexperienced lawyer. Some of his campaigning methods caused concern, though. His statements about his opponent, Judge Edgar Werner, were deliberately misleading. For example, McCarthy portrayed Werner as much older than he was, wondering aloud if the judge were physically fit to be reelected.

Circuit Judge

Joe McCarthy, the youngest judge in Wisconsin at the time, was surrounded by controversy from the beginning of his term. In one case, he actually oversaw the destruction of records he thought were useless. When the case was appealed and the state supreme court learned that the records no longer existed, McCarthy was reprimanded, but not punished, for his actions. In divorce cases, which he granted without delay, he was accused of failing to make couples try to solve their differences. This was a serious charge in the 1940s, when divorce was not acceptable in polite society.

Even so, McCarthy was a popular judge, and his hard work was noted and appreciated. When he took office, his court had a backlog of about two hundred fifty cases. To deal with this problem, McCarthy held court twelve hours a day. During one hectic period, he managed to try forty cases in forty days. Instead of making plaintiffs and defendants come to his courtroom, McCarthy held court in many of the small towns in his district. Between cases, he visited with local citizens, impressing them with his friendliness. Newspaper editors praised his work. One said that Judge McCarthy "administered justice promptly and with a combination of legal knowledge and good sense."[2]

Tailgunner Joe

Biographers of McCarthy have long debated whether he took a leave of absence from his courtroom during World War II for political gain or out of a sense of duty to his country. McCarthy was exempt from service because he was a judge. However, he had long noted how popular war heroes were with voters, and he wanted to advance in politics, though exactly what position he had in mind at this point is not clear. McCarthy decided to enlist in the Marines shortly after America entered the war. He began his tour of duty in the Pacific in August 1942.

To maintain his public image, McCarthy sent reports of his activities to his hometown newspaper. Interest in his exploits soared when Wisconsinites learned that McCarthy had become a tailgunner, the man who rode in the back of a bomber and sprayed bullets at the enemy. He actually set a record, firing off forty-seven hundred rounds of ammunition in one day. Voters were impressed with this accomplishment, not knowing that he had fired most of these rounds at coconut trees on the ground for target practice. In the spring of 1944, McCarthy announced he was running for the United States Senate. Wisconsin's Alexander Wiley, a Republican, was up for re-election. McCarthy planned to challenge him in the primary for the right to be the Republican nominee.

McCarthy's announcement surprised many people. First of all, he had long considered himself a Democrat, not a Republican. Critics of McCarthy believe that he became a Republican because it would increase his chances of winning in a state that was becoming more

Republican by the day. Also, McCarthy was still in the Marines, and servicemen were not allowed to speak out on political issues. This was a serious handicap for a politician. Furthermore, he was still a judge. To keep politics out of the courtroom, Wisconsin law forbids judges from running for any political office.

Despite all of this, McCarthy entered the primary. Supporters at home set up a campaign headquarters, financed by donations and McCarthy's impressive profits from a stock market fund. He had given most of his savings to a friend to invest for him while he was in the service. The investment had paid off well. When it came to light that McCarthy had spent at least twenty thousand dollars of his own money on his campaign, his supporters were alarmed. Candidates were limited to five thousand dollars each. Charges of campaign fraud would haunt him throughout his political career.

Besides running the headquarters, supporters spoke for McCarthy until he could return to Wisconsin. In July, McCarthy's Marine unit was finally transferred to San Diego, California. McCarthy was then given a fifteen-day leave, and he immediately left for his home state and the campaign trail. He got around the problem of servicemen not taking political positions in public very easily. McCarthy simply announced that if he could speak out, this is what he would say, and then he launched into his speech.

McCarthy did not worry about the legality of his candidacy. He knew that he would not beat Senator Wiley, a popular and effective politician with many years of experience in the legislature. McCarthy was only running to gain experience in organizing a campaign and to make people more aware of his name. Once the election was over, McCarthy believed, correctly, no one would file charges against him.

Senator McCarthy

Joe McCarthy accepted his loss in 1944 with grace and set his sights on winning the other Wisconsin Senate seat, then held by Robert LaFollette, Jr. LaFollette, a Republican, would be up for re-election in 1946. He was from a powerful political dynasty that had produced the best-known and most respected leaders in Wisconsin. Few politicians besides McCarthy would even have thought of challenging this elder statesman in his own party. Many Wisconsinites were actually amused by McCarthy's belief that he could unseat the senator in the primary.

Even LaFollette failed to take McCarthy seriously. The senator counted on his legislative record to win votes for him, and he did not return to the state to talk to voters until ten days before the primary was held.

Meanwhile, LaFollette's supporters were restless. They were becoming increasingly fearful of the Soviet Union and the growing estrangement between the free world and the Communists. They wondered if current representatives were able to deal with such a volatile situation. Also, taxpayers were angry about the addition of three hundred thousand government employees to the federal payroll in only seven years. As a result, voters were looking for change.

While LaFollette remained in the nation's capital, McCarthy appeared before every group that asked him to speak. He reminded Wisconsinites of his judicial background and his World War II service in the Marines. He told audiences about his hazardous tour of duty in the Pacific, during which, he said, he had been wounded. McCarthy had, in fact, been injured. However, it was the result of a misstep at a party, not enemy fire. In any event, thirty-seven-year-old McCarthy had so much appeal to the Wisconsin voters that he easily won the race.

McCarthy's upset received lots of attention from the press. Having defeated such a strong candidate as LaFollette in the primary, McCarthy was nearly guaranteed his victory in the general election, when he ran against Democrat Howard McMurray. McCarthy carried seventy of seventy-three counties in the state. He was now on his way to Washington—to fulfill his dream of doing something big.

TREASON!

Though Wisconsinites had high hopes for Joe McCarthy, he failed to distinguish himself during his first years in the Senate. He went from one cause to another without much thought or conviction. He repeatedly angered other senators with his cutting remarks, and his outbursts offended so many senators that some actually refused to chair a committee if he was to be a member. Worst of all, at least for a politician, he had failed to capture the press's attention.

McCarthy was well aware that his re-election hopes were in danger. So for months, he had been looking for an issue he could use to get support and attention. The strong reaction to his speech in Wheeling convinced him that communism was the issue for which he had been searching.

To make the most of his newly found attention, McCarthy scheduled a speech in the Senate shortly after he returned from Wheeling. Wary senators were divided over how best to deal with his presentation.

The Democrats, who had been in control of the federal government for eighteen years, were deeply offended by McCarthy's charges. Afraid of more attacks, these senators tried to find some parliamentary maneuver to keep him from speaking. Failing to do so, many decided to boycott his presentation.

Some Republicans were also afraid of what McCarthy might say. They were not opposed to attacking the Democrats. They just wanted it done in a way that did not bring shame upon the Senate. These Republicans could not prevent McCarthy from speaking either, so they, too, decided to leave when he took the floor.

On the other hand, a few Republican senators were quite willing to hear his case. If it proved to be true, they reasoned, it could be a powerful issue to use against the Democrats in upcoming elections. Besides, some were really convinced that the State Department was riddled with Communists who shaped United States foreign policy in favor of the Soviets. McCarthy, they thought, might be able to get the Reds out.

On the Attack

McCarthy took the Senate floor at 5:00 P.M. on February 20, 1950. For two hours, he talked about communism in general, and he gave what he claimed was the text of his Wheeling speech. He then started to present his list of suspects, using numbers instead of names, describing them only in the most general terms. He did not provide evidence.

Democrats tried to distract McCarthy by interrupting him with questions. This tactic backfired because it angered the Republicans, most of whom now felt the need to protect one of their own. As a result, McCarthy picked up support that he might not have had if the Democrats had not tried to silence him.

At 7:30, McCarthy decided that his information was so important that a quorum, the number of senators needed to conduct official business, should be present. He then demanded that the sergeant at arms round up as many missing senators as possible.

When the chamber was full, McCarthy presented the rest of his suspects. He was working from a list compiled by Robert E. Lee, a former FBI agent who had worked for the State Department's loyalty board. This list had been presented to the House of Representatives several years before. It contained many suspicions but little evidence, and as a result, the House had generally ignored it. Lee had produced 205 names, the number McCarthy had first used when he made his accusations. However, 108 of these "risks" had left the State Department, and only 57 remained in 1948. Now, in 1950, this number had been further reduced. Several anti-Communists provided tips about other risks, and after McCarthy added these names to the list, he had a total of 81 suspects.

For almost four hours, the Senate listened to McCarthy's charges. To try to disguise his source of information, which he falsely claimed had been produced at great risk, he switched the order of the names. He also greatly exaggerated the information that Lee had found.

The presentation of little more than rumors stunned the senators. It was, according to Senator Robert Taft, "a perfectly reckless performance."[1]

Even so, McCarthy's accusations made headlines and frightened the public. Journalists of the day reported news as it happened without questions or comments. As a result, many readers, if they did not read the editorials in the same paper, assumed that McCarthy's charges were the truth. Some did not realize that what a senator said on the Senate floor, no matter how wrong it might be, was protected from the threat of lawsuits. This privilege was established to promote a free exchange of ideas. Once in a while, though, instead of debating issues, a senator took advantage of the privilege, attacking opponents without having to worry about the consequences.

Because many Americans were voicing support for McCarthy, the Senate had little choice but to investigate his charges. To refuse to do so would give the impression that it had something to hide—namely, Communists in the State Department.

The Tydings Committee

The Senate established a five-member committee to investigate McCarthy's charges. This committee consisted of two Democrats, Theodore Green and Brien McMahon, and two Republicans, Henry Cabot Lodge and Bourke Hickenlooper. It was headed by Millard Tydings, a powerful Democrat from Maryland.

McCarthy knew the committee would soon learn that he was working from the Lee list, which had been discredited in 1948. Without more proof, the committee would tear his case apart. So with the help of investigators, he frantically searched for new names and more information about those on the list. One of his main sources for potential security risks was a file compiled by HUAC. This file contained the names of twenty-two thousand suspects. Sympathetic newspaper reporters also gave him a name or two from their files, as did some former Communists.

Eventually McCarthy received so much information that he became physically overwhelmed with the task before him. This affected his health. He complained about recurring stomach pains. A heavy drinker in the past, McCarthy began to consume more alcohol than ever before.

When the Tydings Committee first met on March 8, 1950, the room was full of newspaper reporters and curious spectators. They had come to watch what many thought would be the end of McCarthy.

Tydings had prepared many questions that he believed would embarrass McCarthy. Not wanting to waste time, as soon as McCarthy began to speak, Tydings interrupted him. Tydings asked if McCarthy could name the State Department officer he claimed was responsible for clearing the suspect identified as number fourteen. When McCarthy hemmed and hawed, Tydings repeated his question. "Do you or do you not know the name of this man?" McCarthy shrugged his shoulders, as if it did not matter, then replied, "At this point, Mr. Chairman, I could not give you the names of half of these people."[2]

Other senators might have been embarrassed, but McCarthy's shortage of proof did not stop him. He simply went on to make more accusations. So Tydings continued to interrupt. The chairman's approach eventually offended the Republicans on the committee, and they rallied to McCarthy's defense. A heated exchange followed, and when it ended, McCarthy was the victor. From then on, he was allowed to speak without interruption.

After two weeks of failed attempts to prove that any of his suspects were Communists, McCarthy decided to risk everything on a man he called "the top espionage agent" in the United States. On March 22, McCarthy said, "I am willing to stand or fall on this one. If I am shown to be wrong on this, I think the [committee] would be justified in not taking my other cases too seriously."[3]

The Lattimore Case

Joe McCarthy's "top espionage agent" was Owen Lattimore, a professor and the author of many books and articles about Asia. He had also served as America's political advisor to Chiang Kai-shek in the early 1940s. Lattimore was convinced that Chiang Kai-shek could not win the civil war against the Communists in China, and questioned America's decision to supply him with arms. This upset Chiang Kai-shek's supporters in the United States and raised suspicions about Lattimore's loyalties.

To get the most attention and support for his case, McCarthy made his accusations against Lattimore not only in front of the Tydings Committee but from the Senate floor as well. Only thirty-six senators listened to his speech, but the galleries were full of spectators. McCarthy told the hushed crowd that Lattimore was a Soviet agent and a member of the Communist party. He accused Lattimore of being one of the people who helped deliver China to the Communists. McCarthy then claimed that he had a secret witness and a letter written by Lattimore himself to support his accusations. McCarthy was attacked by irate Democrats. Senator Herbert Lehman pointed out the one-sidedness of the scene before him, saying, "You are making a spectacle to the galleries here and to the public where a man accused has no chance to answer."[4]

Lehman then asked to see Lattimore's letter, so McCarthy invited him to come to his desk. When Lehman did so, McCarthy changed his mind. He refused to let Lehman see the document. Instead, he told his challenger to go back to his seat.

Understandably, tensions were running pretty high when Owen Lattimore appeared before the Tydings Committee on April 6, 1950. The room where the hearing was held was filled with reporters, and others stood in the hall, hoping to catch some of Lattimore's testimony.

Lattimore began with a carefully prepared speech in which he vigorously defended his position on China and argued that he had never been anything but a loyal American. He also attacked McCarthy. Lattimore called him a "willing tool" of the China lobby and, referring to forces behind HUAC, called McCarthy "the simple dupe [puppet] of a group of fanatical persons who have been thoroughly discredited." Lattimore also said that McCarthy's accusations were "contemptible lies."[5]

Lattimore then provided the committee with evidence to prove his loyalty. He introduced letters of praise from Chiang Kai-shek and a summary of his loyalty review conducted by the FBI. He also produced a copy of the letter that McCarthy had said would prove that Lattimore was a Soviet spy. This letter, written in 1943, discussed events in China. It did not prove that Lattimore was a Soviet agent. Instead, the letter would help to clear Lattimore's name.

Unwilling to give up, McCarthy demanded, as he had before, that President Truman let the committee examine Lattimore's entire loyalty file. Thus far, Truman had refused to do so. He believed that the legislature did not have the right to look at the executive department's files. However, he finally gave in. He was afraid that if he did not, he would be accused of a cover-up. Shortly thereafter, committee members began to sort through the documents.

While the committee examined loyalty files, McCarthy prepared for his next presentation against Lattimore. On April 20, seven hundred people stood outside the Senate caucus room just to get a glimpse of McCarthy's secret witness. The witness turned out to be Louis Budenz, a former high-ranking Communist official in America. Budenz had edited the Communist Party of America's newspaper, the *Daily Worker*. He had left the organization in 1946. From then on, he helped the government identify Communists.

Budenz's information about Lattimore was nothing more than hearsay. Budenz admitted that he had never seen Lattimore at any Communist function. He also could not explain why he had never even mentioned Lattimore's name to the FBI, since the suspect was supposed to be the top spy in the United States.

Clearly McCarthy's case was in trouble, but he still refused to give up. Now he counted on the loyalty files to provide the proof he needed. The committee, however, failed to find enough evidence to formally charge Lattimore or any of the other suspects with being Communist agents. McCarthy then accused the government of destroying incriminating documents.

On July 20, the Tydings committee issued its report. "It is," the report said, "clearly apparent that the charges of Communist infiltration of and influence upon the State Department are false."[6] The two committee Republicans did not support this report. They believed there were many unanswered questions.

Public Reaction

The public also believed that McCarthy was on to something. Many Americans had long suspected that Communists were at work in the United States. After all, for years politicians had insisted that this was happening. Besides, the Soviet Union had vowed to conquer America. What better way than to infiltrate the government? Instead of dismissing McCarthy, many now regarded him as a hero. They sent money—up to one thousand dollars a day—to finance his investigation.

Trouble in Korea

The belief in McCarthy's charges was reinforced by a tragic event thousands of miles away, the Korean conflict. Korea had been divided at the 38th parallel at the end of World War II. North Korea, with help from the Soviets, established a Communist government; South Korea was supported by the United States.

On June 25, 1950, heavily armed North Korean soldiers poured over the 38th parallel in an all-out attempt to take over South Korea by force. South Korea then appealed to the United States and the United Nations (UN) for help.

Americans did not want to see yet another country fall to the Communists. The UN agreed to send troops. All the soldiers, 90 percent of whom were Americans, were put under the command of General Douglas MacArthur, an American war hero who was to report to his Commander-in-Chief, President Truman. The goal of the troops was to drive the Communists out of South Korea.

All did not go easily. The UN troops were not adequately trained for the mission. As a result, the North Koreans continued to advance, and by August they had conquered most of South Korea. However, by early fall, UN troops had regrouped, and MacArthur and his men had driven the North Koreans out of the South and back across the 38th parallel.

Although the original goal had been achieved, the UN and President Truman decided to have the troops press onward. They hoped to drive the Communists out of North Korea and reunite the North and South. In October,

UN troops crossed the 38th parallel. As the troops moved north, they noticed an increasing number of Chinese soldiers. Now Truman feared that a war with China—and perhaps the Soviet Union—was possible. When the North Koreans drove UN soldiers south of the 38th parallel in late November, the UN and President Truman ordered MacArthur to recapture land up to the parallel, which he did by late March 1951, and then stop.

But MacArthur wanted to continue his drive into North Korea, which he saw as a chance to crush communism. He even talked about supporting a possible invasion of China by Chiang Kai-shek. When Truman refused to give MacArthur permission to advance, the general was furious. He sought help from Congress. Senators who had long supported Chiang Kai-shek rushed to MacArthur's side. Truman responded by firing the general for insubordination on April 11, 1951.

A real uproar followed. When MacArthur returned to the United States, he was given a hero's welcome. Many Americans, including McCarthy, thought that Communists in the State Department had somehow managed to stop MacArthur just when he was about to deliver a deadly blow to communism. It was a conspiracy at the highest level, MacArthur's supporters shouted, and they would not rest until they knew who was responsible.

Treason!

At first, most of the public's anger was focused on President Truman. Many actually demanded that he be impeached. But McCarthy thought someone else was responsible for stopping the advance. He announced that the real culprit was Dean Acheson, the secretary of state, who was responsible for foreign policy. Without a shred of proof, McCarthy attacked Acheson from the safety of the Senate floor. He told his stunned audience that Acheson should go home to the Soviet Union for which he had worked so long.

Then in June 1951, McCarthy suddenly changed targets. Instead of hurling insults at the secretary of state, McCarthy took aim at yet another well-known American. He began his assault at a press conference by announcing that he had some new and startling information. He had proof of "a conspiracy so immense and an infamy so black as to dwarf any previous such venture in the history of man."[7] When he named George C. Marshall as the guilty party, even McCarthy's staunchest supporters gasped. A World War II general and former secretary of state, Marshall was a hero to many Americans. However, as the current secretary of defense, he had supported Truman's firing of MacArthur. This, plus the fact that the Soviet Union had gained so much territory while Marshall was secretary of state, made him suspect in McCarthy's eyes.

When McCarthy made his charges on June 14, 1951, again from the Senate floor, few senators attended the session. The galleries, though, were full of spectators and reporters. McCarthy had a prepared text of sixty thousand words, which he intended to read to his audience. It was a strange, difficult-to-understand speech. Sections had been taken from articles written by political science professors. At times, McCarthy did not seem to understand what he was reading. After several hours, his audience abandoned him. All, however, understood what McCarthy was saying: Marshall had willingly helped the Soviets.

Many of McCarthy's supporters feared that he had gone too far, and they worried that his goal of finding Communists was in danger. They should not have worried. McCarthy was far from finished. The hunt for Communists had really just begun.

Chapter 5

FEAR ON THE HOME FRONT

By late 1950, the American public was so afraid of communism that 68 percent wanted to make the Communist party illegal. These Americans pointed to the growing number of spies recently uncovered in the United States, including Ethel and Julius Rosenberg, a husband and wife who were arrested, convicted, and executed for giving military information to the Soviets.

Although Americans thought the Communist party was strong, it was actually very weak. Eleven of its leaders had been arrested in 1948, charged with plotting to overthrow the United States government. Since then, the party had spent most of its time and money defending the accused.

Throughout their trial, the eleven Communist leaders denied that they were planning to overthrow the government. When they were found guilty, they appealed the decision, which was known as the Foley Square case. In 1951, their case reached the United States Supreme

Court. The justices, in a 6–2 decision, upheld the conviction.

Although difficult to do, some Americans continued to defend the right of Communists to exist in a democracy. Civil rights lawyers and staunch defenders of the First Amendment pointed out that there was a big difference between talking about destroying the government and taking steps to do it.

Defenders worried about wide-scale investigations. Such actions, lawyers said, would cast suspicion on many, destroying people's reputations and lives. Many of the suspects would lose their jobs. Few—if any—companies wanted Communist employees. In fact, supporters of the right of Communists to exist in America were as terrified of McCarthy as the general public was of communism.

Despite opposition, Senator McCarthy's search for Communists continued. McCarthy attacked individuals and organizations without proof. If someone rose to defend these victims, he lashed out at the defenders, accusing them of being Communists, pinks, or punks. The more fear he raised, the more headlines he grabbed and the more people believed him. His methods were given a name: "McCarthyism."

1950 Elections

McCarthyism played an important role in the 1950 fall elections. Republicans knew the public was concerned about the Red threat, and they made the most of it. They insisted that they alone could protect the nation. Although

Republicans did not win as many election contests as they wanted, they still pulled off some stunning upsets.

One of these upsets took place in Maryland, where Senator Tydings was running for re-election. Tydings, a Democrat, was thought to be unbeatable. He easily won the primary in his party, and he faced a little-known Republican opponent, John Butler, in the general election. Ever since the Tydings Committee had announced that there was no evidence to support McCarthy's accusations about Communists in the government, however, McCarthy had been looking for a way to get back at the committee's chairman. McCarthy decided that the best way to do this was to participate in the senator's defeat.

McCarthy's campaign for John Butler enraged the Democrats. McCarthy crisscrossed the state to speak on behalf of the Republican candidate, claiming that the Democrats and Communists were so much alike in their beliefs that the Democrats should call themselves "Commiecrats."[1] McCarthy also raised large sums of money to finance Butler's campaign, money Tydings's supporters believed came from questionable sources.

The most upsetting event, however, was the publication of a controversial newsletter written by McCarthy's staff. This letter included a photograph of Tydings talking to a Communist party leader, Earl Browder. The photo was a composite of two pictures, one of Tydings and another of Browder, that had been put together to create a scene that had never taken place. Even though the caption beneath the photo clearly stated that the picture was a composite, few people read the fine print. Many assumed Tydings was sympathetic to Communists, just as McCarthy had intended.

On election day, John Butler won by more than forty thousand votes. Many reporters credited Joseph McCarthy with the senator's defeat. He took great satisfaction in Tydings's loss.[2]

McCarthy was also given credit for Senator Scott Lucas's defeat in Illinois. Lucas, who led the Democratic charge against McCarthy when he first spoke to the Senate about Communists in the State Department, was second only to Tydings on McCarthy's hit list. To help defeat Lucas, McCarthy toured the state on behalf of the Republican candidate, Everett Dirksen. Local politics probably had as much to do with Lucas's loss as did McCarthy. Even so, McCarthy was now looked upon as a very powerful man, one few wanted to cross.

Another Senate Committee

When the final votes had been counted in the 1950 election, the public's support for men and women who took the Red threat seriously was obvious. As a result, with an eye on future elections, one of the Senate's first acts of business in 1951 was to create the Internal Security Subcommittee, headed by Pat McCarran.

McCarran firmly believed that something was amiss in the State Department and that the Tydings Committee had not done its job. So McCarran's committee started by reexamining old cases, including the case of Owen Lattimore. After twelve days of questioning, Lattimore was accused of perjury, or lying under oath. Lattimore seemed ill at ease, and his lack of confidence further convinced the public that Tydings's report was a cover-up. This, in turn, resulted in even more public support for McCarthy.

Loyalty Boards

Loyalty boards watched McCarran's committee review old cases with great interest. Believing that past board members had also failed to do their job properly, many boards took another look at previous cases. After some debate, boards changed their guidelines. From then on, members no longer had to provide proof of wrongdoing. Instead, members would determine if a reasonable doubt about the suspect's loyalty existed. This was much easier to establish.

Un-American Activities

While the Senate investigated the State Department and loyalty boards examined old records of federal employees, HUAC also held hearings. This committee, in existence since 1938, was now headed by John Wood.

As had the HUAC committee of 1947–1948, the 1951–1952 committee decided to root out Communists in Hollywood. Writers, directors, and actors who were thought to have Communist ties were brought before the committee for questioning.

An appearance before HUAC was reason enough to be listed in a publication called *Red Channels.* This list included the names of all people in the entertainment industry who had come under suspicion. Written by three former FBI agents, *Red Channels* was a blacklist, used to prevent businesses from hiring those deemed unacceptable by the makers of the list. Afraid that a film or television program might be boycotted by the public if a Communist wrote the script or appeared in the production, advertisers, agents, and producers checked *Red Channels* before accepting plays from any writers or before hiring performers. As a result, those listed could not find work.

The only way suspects could redeem themselves was to name other suspects. Although one screenwriter appeared with a list of one hundred names, many refused to put their friends, past or present, in danger. Actress Lillian Hellman was one of them. She said,

> I am not willing, now or in the future, to bring bad trouble to people who . . . were completely innocent of any talk or any action that was disloyal or subversive. . . . [To] hurt innocent people . . . in order to save myself is, to me, inhuman and indecent and dishonorable.[3]

To avoid testifying and incriminating others, suspects such as Hellman cited the Fifth Amendment. This amendment states that Americans cannot be forced to give evidence that can be used against them. "Taking the fifth," as it is known, infuriated the committee, which responded by charging the suspects with contempt. They would then face a trial, and if found guilty, they could be fined and even imprisoned.

Although the committee was charged only with gathering as much information as possible about the threat of communism, HUAC took it upon itself to punish suspects by making their names public. The committee believed that this would humiliate the suspects and disable any Red threat by scaring off would-be party members.

After investigating Hollywood, HUAC took testimony regarding Communists in the legal profession. Any lawyer who had defended a Communist in court was suspect. Most of these, because they thought the committee's work was un-American, proved to be difficult witnesses. Ben Margolis, who had defended several Hollywood stars, announced, "I have nothing but contempt for this Committee, and I will show it as long as I am up here."[4]

HUAC also investigated labor unions. It was no secret that labor unions had Communist members. In the early days of the labor movement, unions had recruited Communist organizers. Trained by the party, these organizers were bold, aggressive, and deeply committed to the welfare of workers. The organizers were also experienced speakers who could sway crowds, lead meetings, and rally members. They were not afraid of potential violence during a strike.

After World War II, America experienced a wave of strikes, some of which were blamed on Communist influences. By 1947, the public's patience with strikers was exhausted. The American people demanded action. Congress responded by passing the Taft-Hartley Act. Besides putting limits on strikes that affected national security, this act required union leaders to sign statements declaring their loyalty to the United States. Although the loyalty oaths drove many Communists out of the labor movement, some remained. Now HUAC was determined to unmask them.

SECURITY LAWS

ACT	PROVISIONS
HATCH ACT (1939)	Made it illegal for the federal government to hire Communists
SMITH ACT (1940)	Made it unlawful for any person to advocate the overthrow of the United States government by force or to organize or join any group dedicated to the over-throw of the government
McCARRAN ACT (1950)	Made Communist organiza-tions register with the federal government; forbade defense plants from hiring Communists; denied passports to members of Communist organizations
COMMUNIST CONTROL ACT (1954)	Punished organizations with Communist ties, such as unions, by denying them rights other groups enjoyed, including col-lective bargaining

The United States Congress passed legislation trying to limit the threats of communism.

The fear of potential hearings pitted union members against each other. Some did not want to push Communists out of their union, realizing how much these organizers had contributed to the labor movement. Yet if Communists remained, the union could be harassed by HUAC. Worse yet, starting in 1954, when the Communist Control Act would go into effect, any union with Communist members would lose its right to negotiate with management for higher salaries.

Sharing Witnesses

Loyalty boards and Congress were so intent on finding Communists that between early 1950 and the end of 1953, more than one hundred different investigations would be started by Congress alone. In addition, states were encouraged to start their own un-American activities boards. There was often a great demand for former Communists who were willing to help the investigators. As a result, special committees had to be formed to work out schedules to avoid conflicts.

Expel McCarthy!

Meanwhile, Senator Tydings persuaded the Senate to investigate McCarthy's actions in the election in Maryland. A committee did so, and four months later, it called McCarthy's activities dishonest and malicious. However, there was no mention of punishment.

Senator William Benton, a Democrat, was deeply upset by the committee's failure to punish McCarthy. Benton asked the Senate to form yet another committee to look into the issue of whether McCarthy should be expelled from the Senate in light of his activities in the election. Not one senator supported Benton on the Senate floor. They remembered only too well what had happened to Senators Tydings and Lucas for opposing McCarthy, and the senators' fear of losing their own positions forced them to remain silent.

Benton's request might have been forgotten if McCarthy had not come out swinging. He called Benton "the hero of every crook and Communist in and out of government."[5] A few days later, he accused unnamed senators of having Communists on their staffs.

The Senate was furious. Shortly after, it started the Gillette Committee, which was charged with making a recommendation about McCarthy's expulsion. This committee was still at work when the 1952 presidential election took place.

1952 Election

Joe McCarthy was up for re-election in 1952, and because he had made so many headlines, his was one of the most closely watched campaigns in the country. Between bouts of illness and two operations, McCarthy spoke to enthusiastic audiences in Wisconsin.

At the same time, opponents were gathering information to wage war on him on two fronts. They wanted to defeat McCarthy at the voting booth if possible. If that effort failed, they would try to provide the Gillette Committee with enough information to persuade the Senate to expel him.

McCarthy campaigned on only one issue in the primary: the threat of communism. He won by a large margin. After the vote was in, the *Milwaukee Journal*, in a now famous editorial by Paul Ringler, talked about what it meant to have McCarthy run in the general fall election:

> This is not only appalling—it is frightening. It betrays a dulled moral sense, a dimmed instinct for truth, for honor, decency and fairness. It rewards falsehood, chicanery [trickery], deception, ruthlessness, the tactics of smear and fear, and contempt for the constitutional principles that safeguard American human and legal rights.[6]

The editorial had little effect. Newspaper reporters canvassed the voters before the general election to see if McCarthy could beat his rival. When one reporter asked a Wisconsinite if he would vote for McCarthy, the voter said, "Sure, I'm for McCarthy. I'm against communism. He's the only one doing anything about the Communists."[7]

McCarthy's efforts were not limited to his own campaign. He spoke out against Connecticut's Senator Benton, who was also trying to retain his Senate seat. McCarthy called Benton a "mental midget."[8] Then he threatened him, reminding Benton about Tydings's loss in Maryland: "Benton will learn that the people of Connecticut do not like Communists and crooks in government any more than the people of Maryland like them."[9]

On election day, the Republicans won a majority in the House and the Senate as well as the presidency. McCarthy was among the winners. Senator Benton, who lost his bid, joined Tydings and Lucas as some of McCarthy's most prominent victims.

The efforts of the Gillette Committee fizzled soon after. Some members resigned, while others were afraid to tackle McCarthy. The committee also failed to find the evidence that it knew it needed to convince the Senate to expel one of its own. When Congress held its opening session, a smiling and confident Senator Joe McCarthy took his seat.

HUAC Goes Back to Work

After the 1952 election, the Communist issue was so hot that 185 out of the 221 Republican representatives in the House volunteered to serve on HUAC when Congress resumed in January 1953. This time the committee was headed by Harold Velde. His targets were universities and churches.

As early as 1938 when HUAC was started, college professors had attacked the committee. They believed that hunting down people for their political beliefs would make people fearful about expressing their ideas, even in a classroom. Since the exchange of ideas is a major goal of education, professors felt threatened. When they spoke out, HUAC responded by calling them pinks, or worse yet, accused them of teaching communism in the classroom and ruining young minds.

The 1953–1954 committee began its investigation of schools by asking faculty members who had been members of the party in the past to testify. Most of these former members stated that being a Communist might affect what an instructor would teach. The committee set out to find the enemy. The committee formed subcommittees and held numerous hearings, ordering thousands of teachers—an estimated three thousand were already regarded as suspects—to appear for questioning. Many of the educators, including those who took the Fifth Amendment, were fired.

To reduce the threat of communism in all schools, administrators all across the country swung into action. Some states required teachers to take loyalty oaths. Many school systems reviewed textbooks. Any book that mentioned anything that was thought to even vaguely resemble Communist party ideas was removed from schools. In some cases, book reviewers asked publishers to assure them that Communists had not had a part in writing the books. The hunt for Reds then spread to the publishing business.

The committee of 1953–1954 also looked for Communists in churches. Chairman Velde was concerned about the role clergymen were playing in the drive for world peace and civil rights in the United States. Both issues were long-standing goals of the Communists. One especially, peace, would mean cooperating with the Soviets. This was more than HUAC could accept.

The committee began by attacking G. Bromley Oxnam, the Methodist bishop of Washington, D.C. He was also one of the leaders of the World Council of Churches and a vocal critic of HUAC. He was singled out by Congressman Donald Jackson, who said that Oxnam "served God on Sunday and the Communist front for the balance of the week."[10]

Although the public was willing to believe that Communists were at work in the State Department, unions, and even the schools, it could not believe Communists were preaching from the pulpits on Sunday. HUAC's latest charges made Americans take a more thoughtful look at the committee. When they did, they began to question the investigations. The committee then backed off, and only a few clergymen were investigated.

Staying Out of Trouble

As if committees did not have a long enough list of suspects, they were given more names by the attorney general. Attorney General J. Howard McGrath had started a list in 1949, and the attorneys general who followed him in office added to it. The list consisted of Communist front organizations. These groups were usually dedicated to international peace or civil rights. The organizations were founded by Communists, although this information was kept from members. The fronts were a way for the party to promote its goals and to look for new recruits. Belonging to one of these groups, buying a novel in their bookstores, or even attending one of their lectures made one a suspect. This was known as guilt by association. When the list was published, Americans who wanted to stay out of trouble avoided the suspect organizations.

McCarthy Gears for Battle

Even though many were now involved in the war on communism, McCarthy did not stop his attacks. He continued to charge the State Department with harboring Communists. He even attacked the department for some of the library books it carried in its foreign offices. Then, without warning, he changed targets. In late 1953, he zeroed in on a new enemy—the United States Army.

6 Chapter

AT WAR

Up until 1953, Joe McCarthy simply found suspects. He expected the investigative committees or the Senate itself to find proof of wrongdoing. When they failed to do so, he attacked them. His tirades got a lot of attention, especially when he accused the Democrats of "twenty years of treason."[1] This charge was repeated by Republican candidates, and it became a powerful political weapon in the 1952 election.

In early 1953, however, some Republicans believed that McCarthy might become a problem for the party if he continued to make charges without proof. These men wanted to muzzle him. So McCarthy was asked to chair the Government Operations Committee. This committee was supposed to study government waste, a big task. Republicans believed that McCarthy's new position would keep him busy and out of the headlines. Majority Leader Robert Taft bragged, "We've got McCarthy where he can't do any harm."[2]

Taft, however, underestimated Joe McCarthy. The committee he was to chair had subcommittees as well. These included the little-known Subcommittee on Investigations, which had few limits on what it could study. Armed with Senate financing, McCarthy hired anti-Communist staff members for the subcommittee. They were as determined as he was to find Reds.

One of these members, Roy Cohn, had an impressive legal background and, according to McCarthy, an outstanding anti-Communist record. Cohn had helped the prosecution in the famous Foley Square case, the result of which was the imprisonment of eleven Communist leaders. Cohn had also helped the prosecution win its case against Ethel and Julius Rosenberg, both of whom were convicted of being Soviet spies and executed in 1953.

Another member of McCarthy's staff was Gerard Schine. Roy Cohn considered Schine indispensable. So in the fall of 1953, when Schine was drafted into the army, Cohn was very upset. Somehow, Cohn managed to convince the army that Schine's services were needed on McCarthy's staff. As a result, Schine was given special privileges. For example, he received almost unlimited passes so that he could leave his base in New Jersey to attend committee meetings.

With more power than ever and a supportive committee behind him, McCarthy ran wild. He held 445 preliminary inquiries and 157 investigations in the first year alone.

An Attack on the Army Signal Corps

One of McCarthy's investigations in 1953 involved the Army Signal Corps at Fort Monmouth in New Jersey. McCarthy and his committee, after only a few months of interviewing witnesses, thought they had discovered a Communist operation. To get the most attention possible for his latest charges, McCarthy arranged to create a scene guaranteed to capture headlines. After he received a prearranged message from Cohn, McCarthy would rush back to Washington from the British West Indies, where he was honeymooning with his bride, Jean Kerr McCarthy. This required a great deal of understanding on the part of Mrs. McCarthy. However, she had been a member of McCarthy's staff, and she supported her husband's work wholeheartedly.

Fort Monmouth was a research and development center for the army as well as a base for soldiers. It had been investigated by both the FBI and HUAC in 1952, after classified documents had disappeared. Neither investigation had turned up evidence of Communist spies, but both indicated that security measures were sloppy.

When he was called back to Washington to supposedly examine new information that his committee had found, McCarthy, as expected, was eventually surrounded by reporters. He told them that he had proof of "extremely dangerous espionage" that could "envelop the whole Signal Corps."[3]

The subcommittee then scheduled closed-door meetings with witnesses. Once in a while, McCarthy would leave the sessions to give reporters his version of what was happening. His reports were full of news about spies. The hearings continued for weeks in order to question more than fifty people suspected of spying for the Soviets.

The army, eager to avoid a confrontation with McCarthy, helped the subcommittee in any way it could, questioning suspects as well. The procedures were highly irregular, and suspects' legal rights were ignored. All of those questioned were suspended without pay until their innocence could be proven. None was provided with the names of his or her accusers. None was able to examine the evidence against him or her. Some were questioned because one or two of their classmates in college were known Communists. One man was a suspect because his father was thought to be a Soviet sympathizer. Another was accused of being a Red because he attended a Communist party meeting with his parents when he was twelve years old.

In the end, neither the army nor the committee could prove that any of the suspects, mostly civilians, had been Communist spies. Although almost all of the victims got their jobs back, a few had to fight for years to clear their names and get their back pay.

While McCarthy was grilling suspects at Fort Monmouth, the army announced that Schine would soon be sent to Georgia and then perhaps overseas. Cohn and McCarthy saw this as an attempt to hamper and even discourage further investigations. The struggle over where Schine would serve continued for months. Cohn eventually threatened to wreck the army and drive Secretary of the

Army Robert Stevens from office if Schine was made unavailable. Exactly how Cohn planned to do this is not clear, for he did not follow through when Schine was assigned to a base in Georgia. Even though the army held its ground in the end, Secretary Stevens was embittered by the skirmish over Schine. Eventually, Stevens would play an important part in McCarthy's downfall.

An Attack on the White House

When the Republicans took over in 1952 and Dwight Eisenhower became the president, they promised Americans that they would find and dismiss Reds in the government. By the autumn of 1953, when the Fort Monmouth hearings were taking place, the government had removed more than two thousand federal employees. Attorney General Herbert Brownell used the numbers, plus some new charges about Communists in the White House under Truman, to show how lax the Democrats had been regarding the Red threat.

In a televised broadcast, Truman denied knowingly hiring any Communists. He wanted to know how many of the two thousand former employees were security risks. Truman also accused Brownell of McCarthyism.

McCarthy, appearing to be deeply offended about the negative use of his name, demanded airtime to respond to Truman. The senator attacked the former president, claiming that Truman's administration had been full of Communists. Many Americans agreed.

McCarthy then attacked his own party's leader, President Dwight Eisenhower. Tired of McCarthyism,

Eisenhower had stated that he hoped the issue of communism would not play a part in the elections of 1954. McCarthy, who did not want to give up such a popular issue, informed the president that "The raw, harsh, unpleasant fact is that Communism is an issue and it will be an issue in 1954. . . . Practically every issue we face today, from high taxes to the shameful mess in Korea, is . . . interwoven with the Communist issue."[4]

McCarthy went on to discuss his party's failure to end the Red threat and wondered aloud why President Eisenhower permitted John Davies, once a member of the State Department, to remain in the government. Davies had been an advisor in China, where he had criticized American support for Chiang Kai-shek. This made him, as well as his supporters, suspect.

Personnel in the White House were stunned by McCarthy's performance. Shortly thereafter, some Republicans, including Vice President Richard Nixon, began a series of talks with McCarthy. They were afraid that he would split the Republican party between the diehards who supported McCarthyism and those who had tired of the issue. A split would weaken the party and potentially result in losses in the 1954 election. Nixon and the others wanted to work out a compromise.

Some Republicans, on the other hand, were too angry to compromise. They wanted to cut McCarthy's funding and vote his committee out of existence. Eventually, McCarthy agreed to cut back on his investigations of suspected spies and look at other issues. In exchange, his funding would continue.

The Republican senators and the White House staff congratulated themselves on the deal, believing that their limits on McCarthy would gain support and respect from the public. They were shocked when polls taken in January 1954 revealed that McCarthy's support had climbed 16 percent in the last few months. Now 50 percent of Americans supported his fight against communism. In fact, 40 percent of the Democrats thought he was on the right track.

The Army—Again

Joe McCarthy continued making accusations. As before, he was given many tips by supporters. One of these tips concerned an army dentist named Irving Peress.

Peress had been drafted into the army in 1952. Because of his age and training, he entered the service as a captain. When he had finished a year of service, he was automatically promoted to major. Peress had not answered all of the questions, particularly those about loyalty, on his enlistment forms when he was drafted. This was not noticed for months. However, when the army finally discovered the blanks, it decided to remove Peress as quickly as possible rather than raise a ruckus about Peress's loyalty and draw attention to the fact that someone in the army had been careless. The fastest way to do this was to give him an honorable discharge.

Unable to find spies at Fort Monmouth, McCarthy jumped on the Peress case with zeal. He wanted to know who had promoted the dentist and who had given him an honorable discharge. Above all, McCarthy wanted the dentist court-martialed.

To get answers, McCarthy began an investigation into the case in January 1954. Among the witnesses called was Brigadier General Ralph W. Zwicker. McCarthy bullied and insulted Zwicker, telling the World War II hero that he was not fit to wear the uniform of an American soldier.

Secretary of the Army Robert Stevens was so incensed by McCarthy's attacks on Zwicker that he ordered the general not to testify again. When Stevens told McCarthy about this decision, McCarthy shouted, "Just go ahead and try it, Robert. I am going to kick the brains out of anyone who protects Communists! . . . You just go ahead. I will guarantee you that you will live to regret it."[5]

Republican leaders tried to smooth over the rift between McCarthy and the army. When all was said and done, McCarthy managed to get his way. The hearings would continue.

At the same time, though, the army started to put together a case against McCarthy. Secretary Stevens believed McCarthy was behind Cohn's threats regarding Schine's transfer. On March 11, the army released a thirty-four-page report to the press. This report accused McCarthy of intimidating and improperly influencing the army.

McCarthy responded by saying that Stevens was trying to force him to drop his investigation. The army, McCarthy said, had drafted Schine so that it could hold him hostage. If McCarthy did not back off, Schine would be punished.

The Army-McCarthy Hearings

Charges and countercharges flew between the army and McCarthy. To sort out the whole mess, the Senate decided to hold another hearing. Understandably, no one was eager to tangle with either McCarthy or the army. Eventually, the task fell to McCarthy's own committee. McCarthy was replaced as chair by Senator Karl Mundt.

The rules were simple. The committee would call the witnesses and ask the questions. McCarthy, or his lawyer, Ray Jenkins, and the lawyer for the army, Joseph Welch, could cross-examine the witnesses.

The hearings began on March 16, 1954. Hundreds of spectators and reporters crowded into the Senate Caucus Room to witness firsthand a hearing that had been eagerly anticipated. More than 20 million Americans watched the proceedings on television. The hearings, which replaced regular daytime programming, ran for thirty-six days. Few viewers turned away from their televisions, even when what they saw shocked and saddened them.

The army began by giving evidence to back up its claim that it had given Schine special treatment. Schine, for example, was allowed to skip half the time that would normally be spent in basic training. He was excused from routine drills and made or received two hundred fifty long-distance calls. The army then contended that it gave Schine so many privileges because it was threatened by McCarthy.

McCarthy, Cohn, and their lawyer responded with a photograph. It showed Secretary of the Army Robert Stevens and Gerard Schine having a friendly chat. How,

McCarthy wondered aloud, could the army argue that it was intimidated? It gave privileges to Schine, McCarthy said, because it wanted to do so.

Like another famous photo that McCarthy had used several years before, this picture was not quite what it seemed to be. Someone on McCarthy's staff had made a copy of a photo that showed Stevens talking to several people, all of whom were facing him. Schine was part of this group. Whoever altered the photo cut out the figures of Stevens and Schine. These two figures were then placed side by side, facing each other, and a new photo was taken. The result was a picture of two happy people talking to each other.

The army's legal team challenged the photo by producing the original. Even when the two pictures were shown together, McCarthy denied that any cropping had taken place. But the audience could see what had been done. The facial expressions, positions of the heads, and clothing worn were identical to those in the original picture. McCarthy, who had long accused his suspects of lying, was clearly not telling the truth.

McCarthy then presented a letter from the FBI. It supposedly warned the army about Communist spies at Fort Monmouth, which, McCarthy said, was ignored. McCarthy thought this proved that someone in the army was a Communist sympathizer. This letter, like the faked photo, turned out to be a cut-and-paste job. McCarthy had eliminated some parts to create a document that in no way resembled the original. Worse yet, the letter contained classified material that he should not have had. When questioned about how he got the information, McCarthy refused to answer. McCarthy, who had berated witnesses for not answering questions, was now refusing to testify. They were un-American. He considered himself a hero.

The climax came on June 9. The army's lawyer, Joseph Welch, was deliberately baiting Roy Cohn, trying to get him to lose his temper in the hope that he might give incriminating evidence. Welch had been questioning Cohn about a statement he had made regarding running every Communist out of town by sundown. Cohn kept his composure, but McCarthy did not. He rose to tell Welch about a Communist in his own law firm, someone Welch should run out of town, Fred Fisher.

While the audience held its breath, Welch slowly turned to face McCarthy. Welch knew that as a young man Fisher had once belonged to the National Lawyers Guild. Shortly after this organization was judged dangerous by the attorney general, Fisher had resigned. When Fisher was asked to help with the army hearings, he declined. He told Welch about his background. He believed it would hurt Welch's defense of the army if people found out about it. Fisher had been trying to bury his past. Now, because of McCarthy, all of it would become public knowledge. Welch explained the situation and argued that Fisher had suffered enough. He called McCarthy's charge reckless and cruel. Then he added, "Let us not assassinate this lad further, Senator. You have done enough. Have you no sense of decency, sir, at long last? Have you left no sense of decency?"[6] Members of the audience were asking the same question.

The final reports of the committee were issued on August 31. Both sides were criticized. But it would not have really mattered what was said. Millions of television viewers had seen McCarthy in action—lying, snarling, and snapping at committee members, bullying the opposition, and attempting to smear everyone who opposed him. They had watched him repeatedly interrupt the proceedings by shouting "Point of order!" This was supposed to be done only to point out a mistake in procedure. While McCarthy was explaining the so-called mistake, he had a chance to grab the spotlight and give a speech until the chairman made him be quiet. Children thought his actions were funny. They imitated him, running around playgrounds shouting, "Point of order!" Most adults, however, were dismayed by the spectacle. A few were even ready to stand up to McCarthy—no matter what the consequences might be.

JOE MUST GO

After the hearings, even some of Joseph McCarthy's staunchest supporters turned against him. Among them was radio commentator H. V. Kaltenborn, who said that McCarthy had "become completely egotistical, arrogant, arbitrary, narrow-minded, reckless, and irresponsible. Power," the commentator added, "has corrupted him."[1]

While many discussed McCarthy's shortcomings, a few took action either to remove him from the Senate or at least to curb his power. Both groups were led by former McCarthy supporters and Republican senators. Critics and Democrats joined them, but they did not dare to lead the attacks. They would have been labeled Communists by McCarthy if they had, and their efforts would have been questionable in the eyes of the many Americans who still supported the senator.

Recall Drive

One effort to remove McCarthy from the Senate began in his home state. It became known as the "Joe Must Go" campaign. On March 15, 1954, Leroy Gore, the editor of the *Sauk-Prairie Star*, began a recall drive. According to Wisconsin law, an elected official can be forced to run in a special election before his or her term is up if enough dissatisfied voters sign petitions. Gore announced the recall campaign in an editorial. Then he handed out fifteen thousand petitions. He and his supporters had sixty days to get the legally required number of signatures, in this case, four hundred thousand. Gore narrowly missed his goal. Although he did not force the special election, he did demonstrate that many Wisconsinites no longer supported their senator.

Censure in the Senate

Meanwhile, Republicans in the Senate were trying to decide how best to handle McCarthy. Many were now unwilling to put up with his behavior until his term ended in 1959. Some senators wanted to expel him, while others talked about censuring him. To censure a senator was to condemn him for his actions. This was a very serious punishment. Censure would not only mean public humiliation, but would also result in being shunned in the Senate. No one would support or even talk to a censured senator.

On July 30, 1954, Senator Ralph Flanders introduced a resolution to censure McCarthy. The Senate then asked Flanders to make specific charges and present them to a special committee for investigation. This committee was to be headed by Arthur Watkins.

The Watkins Committee established rules to keep the hearing as dignified as possible. Members did not want McCarthy to turn the event into a spectacle. To silence him, the committee decided that witnesses could be questioned by McCarthy or by his lawyer, but not by both. Since McCarthy knew an outburst would only make things worse, he had little choice but to let his lawyer, Edward Bennett Williams, do the talking.

The Watkins Committee decided to take evidence in five areas. Witnesses were to give statements about (1) incidents during which McCarthy had shown contempt for the Senate; (2) events during which he had encouraged federal employees to violate the law by passing on confidential information to him; (3) his receipt of classified information; (4) his abuse of Senate colleagues; and (5) his abuse of General Zwicker.

On September 27, the committee released its unanimous report to the press. It recommended censure for contempt of the Senate and attacks on Zwicker. On November 8, after the fall elections, the report was officially filed with the Senate.

McCarthy could not personally fight the committee at the hearings, but this did not mean he could not fight back. When the Watkins report was filed, McCarthy announced that censure would be a major victory for the Communist party. He insisted that the Reds now had power over United States senators, who were little more than handmaidens of the Soviets.

On November 15, McCarthy, still head of the Subcommittee on Investigations, called Watkins to testify.

McCarthy insulted Watkins when he could not tell the committee who had promoted Peress the dentist. Watkins, who had no way of knowing who promoted whom in the army, was called derelict in his duty and worse. Every time McCarthy opened his mouth, he provided yet another example of his contempt for his colleagues.

The full Senate began its debate on the censure issue on November 16. Senators took the floor to denounce McCarthy. It was not a pretty sight. When the debate ended, the Senate offered a resolution to censure McCarthy on two counts: contempt of the Senate by refusing to appear before the Senate committee investigating his activities in the 1952 election, and his abuse of the Watkins Committee.

On December 2, the Senate voted on the resolutions. Sixty-seven senators voted to censure McCarthy. Twenty-two refused to do so. All of the Democrats voted against him. The Republicans split their vote: twenty-two for and twenty-two against McCarthy. Three senators did not vote: McCarthy, Democrat John F. Kennedy, and Republican Alexander Wiley, the other senator from Wisconsin.

Censure was painful for McCarthy. When he spoke in the Senate, the other senators left the room. If he greeted a senator in the hallway, his greeting was ignored. No one asked McCarthy for help on the campaign trail. Also, censure made it possible for leaders to publicly avoid him. McCarthy was the only senator not welcome in the White House. In addition, few leaders even wanted to be seen with him. When he tried to take a seat next to Vice

President Nixon at a fund-raising event in Wisconsin, Nixon's aides asked McCarthy to move.

No Longer a Threat

McCarthy simply could not understand what had happened. Not only had he lost all influence in the Senate, but after the censure vote only 36 percent of Americans had a favorable impression of him. Over the next few years, he would wonder aloud why his words, which once had influenced millions, no longer had a powerful effect. McCarthy simply refused to look at his methods, which, when repeated over and over, finally turned the Senate and the public against him. He also failed to realize that several events in the world had made the Red menace less threatening abroad and at home.

The first of these events was the death of Soviet leader Joseph Stalin on March 5, 1953. Stalin was replaced by leaders who wanted the Korean conflict to end. Stalin had encouraged the North Koreans to refuse to sign a peace treaty until they had taken more territory. Now, with Soviet encouragement, a truce was declared, and fighting officially ended on July 27, 1953. The Soviets' role in ending the conflict encouraged Americans to believe that a better relationship between the two countries was possible. The end of the Korean conflict proved that Communist expansion could be stopped.

The second event was a dramatic speech given by Nikita Khruschev, who took control of the Soviet Union after Stalin's death. Rumors of Stalin's cruelty were common, but there was little evidence until Khruschev spoke out. In what was supposed to be a secret speech, Khruschev told the Communist Party Congress in early 1956 that Stalin had ordered the arrest of his opponents, real or imagined. Khruschev estimated that thousands had been tortured until they confessed to crimes against the state. Some were imprisoned; others were executed. Khruschev's estimates were low. Today historians believe that perhaps as many as 5 million were killed for their opposition to Stalin.

Copies of Khruschev's speech eventually reached the United States, and the Communist party printed all twenty thousand words in its *New York Daily Worker*. Howard Fast was one of the paper's writers. He spoke for many party members when he said,

> [The speech] shook us violently. There [was] no use in trying to sum up the contents of the speech; it [was] an awful and terrifying list of infamies, murders, tortures, and betrayals. . . . When I first read those twenty thousand words of horror and infamy, I exploded with rage—as did so many others on the staff.[2]

Fast had become a Communist to make life better for the poor and to make America more like Lenin's ideal. Now, after seeing what communism could become, he resigned from the party. So did many others. By 1957, the Communist Party of America had fewer than twenty thousand members, down from thirty thousand in its heyday. The falling membership convinced the public that a Communist threat on the home front had been greatly reduced.

The Last Years

While communism was all but disappearing, in America, McCarthy's health problems increased. He had more sinus infections and stomach problems than ever before. His liver, seriously damaged by infectious hepatitis years before, began to fail. His doctors insisted that he take some time away from the Senate, rest, eat properly, and give up all alcoholic beverages. For a while, McCarthy managed to do this.

When he returned to his old habits, however, he collapsed. On April 28, 1957, he was rushed to Bethesda Naval Hospital in Maryland. The man for whom an era was named died from cirrhosis of the liver on May 2. He was forty-eight years old.

His survivors included his wife, Jean, and their six-month-old adopted daughter, Tierney Elizabeth.

Following funeral services in Washington, D.C., McCarthy's body was flown to Appleton, Wisconsin. More than seventeen thousand Wisconsinites lined the streets of the city to get a glimpse of his coffin as the hearse made its way to St. Mary's Church. He was buried beside his parents in St. Mary's cemetery.

Shortly after McCarthy's death, a few of his most ardent supporters began to question how he died. They believed poison was put into his medication in the hospital by a Communist sympathizer. They wrote elaborate explanations about how it could be done. Even today, a few continue to believe that he was murdered because he was getting too close to the truth to be allowed to live. McCarthy, they argue, was about to identify the most powerful Communist in America. Each year, on May 2, they and other McCarthy followers hold memorial services at his grave.

Victims of McCarthyism

It is impossible to estimate how many Americans were victimized during the McCarthy era. If all the names of those suspects ordered to appear before investigators— federal and state employees, movie stars, lawyers, generals, union members, teachers, and preachers—were tallied, they would certainly number in the thousands. Although not all of them lost their jobs, it is safe to say that many of them did. Few—if any—employers dared to have suspected Communists on their payrolls. The risk of public condemnation and the potential loss of business were simply too great.

In addition to the emotional turmoil of being investigated and the loss of one's job, a suspect was ridiculed by the public and often avoided by friends and acquaintances. It was a nightmare that sometimes seemed to have no end. Some suspects were questioned repeatedly. One man was questioned seventy times by the FBI because he gave ten dollars to a legal defense fund that the FBI thought was suspicious.

Not all victims appeared before boards, however. The search for Reds was sometimes unofficial. Friends, neighbors, and co-workers judged each other. Those thought to be Communists were kept at arm's length. Americans understood that they could get into trouble by simply talking to a Red. How many were victimized by such judgments will never be known.

During the height of McCarthy's power, dissent was thought to be the same thing as treason. As a result, many Americans were so frightened that they stopped speaking their minds. Fear limited debate and discussion so much that some historians have called Americans of the 1950s the Silent Generation. Even though they never appeared before investigators, they, too, were victims.

Another victim of McCarthyism was social reform. Any change was suspect. For example, women in New York trying to organize a day care center for children, a new idea then, were accused of being Communists.

McCarthyism continued to claim victims long after Joseph McCarthy died. The House Committee on Un-American Activities held hearings until 1977, and it regularly issued lists of organizations that it thought were dangerous to America. In addition, many states and the federal government continued to require loyalty oaths well into the 1960s. The John Birch Society, which today has its headquarters in Appleton, Wisconsin, began to hunt down Communists and warn Americans about international plots to undermine America in 1959. Today, some members proudly call themselves "McCarthyites."

Going to Court

Some of the victims fought back, and after years of hearings and appeals, parts of the laws that made it possible to hunt down Communists were overturned. In 1957, for example, the United States Supreme Court struck down part of the Smith Act. Americans, the Court said, have the right to believe anything, and they cannot be denied the right to join a group that believes in the overthrow of the government. There is a significant difference, the Court added, between believing something and doing it.

Almost all of the McCarran Act was declared unconstitutional as well. In decisions in 1964, 1965, and 1968, the justices struck down one provision after another. As a result, Communist groups were no longer required to register with the government. Also, Communists could no longer be denied jobs in the defense industry or denied passports. The Court ruled that the provisions were discriminatory and that they punished American Communists for their beliefs.

Loyalty boards also came under fire. In 1956, the Supreme Court limited their power. In a 6–3 decision, the Court said that people could not simply be labeled a security risk and fired without a proper hearing. They were entitled to face their accusers and examine the evidence. Also, even if a person could be shown to be a loyalty risk, he or she could not be dismissed unless the job was a sensitive one where the security of the United States might be in danger.

In short, much of what Joe McCarthy and his supporters had done was illegal, just as many victims had claimed all along. However, McCarthy got away with violating his victims' right of free speech, among other rights, because the public was so afraid of communism that it supported his investigations. Americans believed that the end, finding Communists, justified the means, McCarthy's ruthless tactics. No one could have realized how many Americans would be hurt or how ineffective McCarthy would be. He failed to find one Communist even though some historians now believe that there really were Communists working for the federal government then. What threat they posed is not clear. However, McCarthy drew so much attention to his antics and innocent suspects that the real Communists went undetected.

The Breakup of the Soviet Union

The end of the Communist menace at home and a thaw in the Cold War after Stalin's death did not automatically mean that America was safe from communism. The Soviet Union still presented a real threat, although it was not as great as Americans thought.

Even though the United States had a sophisticated spy network in the Soviet Union, Americans were not fully aware of all the problems the Communist party faced in the Soviet Union or how weak the country was. The economy never really prospered. Soviet workers eventually tired of sacrificing and toiling for the good of the state and having little themselves to show for their efforts. They bristled with anger when the military, attempting to have at least as powerful a force as the United States, spent millions of dollars developing bigger and more powerful weapons. Soviet citizens wanted more homes, schools, and roads instead. Furthermore, no matter how many opponents of communism were arrested, the desire for freedom never died.

During the 1980s, the countries that the Soviet Union ruled in Eastern Europe began to defy the Soviet government. The Communists either had to use massive military force to try to hold on to these countries or give them their freedom. The Soviets had used military power in the 1950s to put down revolts, and this had led to worldwide condemnation. This time the Soviets decided to just let the countries go.

If freedom was good for Eastern European countries, Soviet citizens said, why wasn't it good for the Soviets? The Communist party, under the leadership of Mikhail Gorbachev, bowed to mounting pressure and decided to give Soviet citizens free and open elections in 1990. Most citizens voted for opponents of communism, and as a result, the party lost its hold on the Soviet Union. So, like the McCarthy era, the Red Scares, and the Cold War, Lenin's dream of a Communist world, with the Soviet Union as its leader, came to an end. Ironically, it came not as a result of Joe McCarthy's efforts, but by the efforts of the Soviets themselves.

☆ TIMELINE ☆

1908—Joseph McCarthy born in Grand Chute, Wisconsin.

1914—World War I begins.

1917—Lenin and his followers seize control of Russia.

1918—World War I ends.

1919—America experiences its first Red Scare.

1924—Lenin dies; The Soviet Union is now led by Joseph Stalin.

1935—McCarthy begins law practice in Waupaca, Wisconsin.

1938—HUAC is established.

1939—McCarthy elected a Wisconsin circuit judge; World War II begins; Hatch Act passed.

1940—Smith Act passed.

1941—United States enters World War II.

1942—McCarthy enters Marine Corps.

1944—McCarthy loses his first United States Senate bid.

1945—World War II ends.

1946—McCarthy elected to the Senate in November.

1947—President Harry Truman starts loyalty boards.

1948—Eleven Communists indicted in July for violating the Smith Act; In August, Whittaker Chambers accuses Alger Hiss of being a Communist.

1949—State Department announces that China will fall to the Communists.

1950—Alger Hiss found guilty in January; Klaus Fuchs arrested for espionage and McCarthy gives his famous speech in Wheeling, West Virginia, in February; North Korea invades South Korea in June; Second Red Scare begins; In July, the Tydings Committee denounces McCarthy's charges; McCarran Act passed.

1951—Truman fires General Douglas MacArthur in April; McCarthy attacks General George Marshall in June; Senator Benton moves to expel McCarthy in August.

1952—McCarthy accuses Democratic candidates of aiding Communists; Republican Dwight Eisenhower elected president and McCarthy reelected to the United States Senate in November.

1953—McCarthy becomes chairman of the Government Operations Committee in January; Stalin dies in March; United States Army drafts Gerard Schine in July; Truce declared in Korea in July; In October, McCarthy begins to seek Reds in the Army Signal Corps.

1954—Army-McCarthy hearings and recall drive in Wisconsin begin in March; Communist Control Act passed; In December, Senate censures McCarthy.

1955—Khruschev becomes leader of the Soviet Union; Membership in the Communist Party of America drops.

1956—United States Supreme Court limits power of loyalty boards.

1957—McCarthy dies on May 2; Supreme Court strikes down part of the Smith Act.

1964—United States Supreme Court strikes down part of the McCarran Act.

1977—HUAC is terminated.

1990—Elections are held in the Soviet Union; The Communist party loses its control of the Soviet Union.

☆ CHAPTER NOTES ☆

Chapter 1. A Most Unusual Beginning

1. Lately Thomas, *When Even Angels Wept* (New York: William Morrow & Company, Inc., 1973), p. 87.

2. Norman K. Risjord, *Wisconsin: The Story of the Badger State* (Madison: Wisconsin Trails, 1995), p. 202.

Chapter 2. Red Scares

1. Roberta Strauss Feuerlicht, *Joe McCarthy and McCarthyism: The Hate That Haunts America* (New York: McGraw-Hill Book Company, 1972), p. 33.

2. Howard Fast, *Being Red* (Boston: Houghton Mifflin Company, 1990), p. 87.

3. Sandor Voros, *American Commissar* (New York: Chilton Company, 1961), p. 252.

4. William H. Chafe, *The Unfinished Journey: America Since World War II* (New York: Oxford University Press, 1991), p. 109.

Chapter 3. Tailgunner Joe

1. David M. Oshinsky, *A Conspiracy So Immense: The World of Joe McCarthy* (New York: The Free Press, 1983), p. 9.

2. Thomas C. Reeves, *The Life and Times of Joe McCarthy: A Biography* (New York: Stein and Day, 1982), p. 35.

Chapter 4. Treason!

1. David M. Oshinsky, *A Conspiracy So Immense: The World of Joe McCarthy* (New York: The Free Press, 1983), p. 114.

2. Ibid., p. 120.

3. Allen J. Matusow, ed., *Great Lives Observed: Joseph R. McCarthy* (Englewood Cliffs, N.J.: Prentice-Hall, Inc., 1970), p. 36.

4. Thomas C. Reeves, *The Life and Times of Joe McCarthy: A Biography* (New York: Stein and Day, 1982), p. 269.

5. Ibid., p. 273.

6. Matusow, p. 39.

7. Robert Griffith, *The Politics of Fear: Joseph R. McCarthy and the Senate*, 2nd ed. (Amherst: The University of Massachusetts Press, 1987), p. 145.

Chapter 5. Fear on the Home Front

1. David M. Oshinsky, *A Conspiracy So Immense: The World of Joe McCarthy* (New York: The Free Press, 1983), p. 175.

2. Thomas C. Reeves, *The Life and Times of Joe McCarthy: A Biography* (New York: Stein and Day, 1982), p. 346.

3. Walter Goodman, *The Committee: The Extraordinary Career of the House Committee on Un-American Activities* (New York: Farrar, Straus and Giroux, 1968), p. 305.

4. Ibid., p. 313.

5. Oshinsky, pp. 219–220.

6. Edwin R. Bayley, *Joe McCarthy and the Press* (Madison: The University of Wisconsin Press, 1981), p. 99.

7. Lately Thomas, *When Even Angels Wept* (New York: William Morrow & Company, Inc., 1973), p. 277.

8. Robert P. Ingalls, *Point of Order: A Profile of Senator Joe McCarthy* (New York: G. P. Putnam's Sons, 1981), p. 71.

9. Thomas, p. 277.

10. Goodman, p. 334.

Chapter 6. At War

1. Roberta Strauss Feuerlicht, *Joe McCarthy and McCarthyism: The Hate That Haunts America* (New York: McGraw-Hill Book Company, 1972), p. 112.

2. Richard M. Fried, *The McCarthy Era in Perspective: Nightmare in Red* (New York: Oxford University Press, 1990), p. 134.

3. Thomas C. Reeves, *The Life and Times of Joe McCarthy: A Biography* (New York: Stein and Day, 1982), p. 517.

4. Ibid., p. 530.

5. Robert Griffith, *The Politics of Fear: Joseph R. McCarthy and the Senate*, 2nd ed. (Amherst: The University of Massachusetts Press, 1987), p. 247.

6. Allen J. Matusow, ed., *Great Lives Observed: Joseph R. McCarthy* (Englewood Cliffs, N.J.: Prentice-Hall, Inc., 1970), p. 95.

Chapter 7. Joe Must Go

1. Roberta Strauss Feuerlicht, *Joe McCarthy and McCarthyism: The Hate That Haunts America* (New York: McGraw-Hill Book Company, 1972), p. 121.

2. Howard Fast, *Being Red* (Boston: Houghton Mifflin Company, 1990), p. 287.

☆ FURTHER READING ☆

Books

Giblin, James Cross. *The Rise and Fall of Senator Joe McCarthy.* New York: Clarion, 2009.

Hakim: Joy. *A History of US: All the People 1945–2001.* New York: Oxford University Press, 2000.

Haynes, Charles C, Sam Chaltain, and Susan M. Glisson. *First Freedoms: A Documentary History of First Amendment Rights in America.* New York: Oxford University Press, 2006.

Sherrow, Victoria. *Notorious Americans: Joseph McCarthy.* Woodbridge, CT: Blackbirch Press, 1998.

Stein, R. Conrad. *The Great Red Scare.* Morristown, NJ: Silver Burdett Press, 1998.

Tracy, Kathleen. *The McCarthy Era.* Hockessin, DE: Mitchell Lane Publishers, 2008.

☆ INDEX ☆